Elements of Music

Class Music Projects for Ages 11-14

Chris Gill

Copyright

© Chris Gill 2015

Pages may be freely photocopied by the purchasing school

Picture credits

All pictures either public domain or reproduced under the Creative Commons Licence

Title page – OpenClipArtVectors https://pixabay.com/p-159870/?no_redirect

Violin – Pianoplonkers https://upload.wikimedia.org/wikipedia/commons/f/f4/German,_maple_Violin.JPG

Viola – Just plain Bill https://upload.wikimedia.org/wikipedia/commons/c/cd/Bratsche.jpg

Cello - Georg Feitscher https://en.wikipedia.org/wiki/Cello#/media/File:Cello_front_side.png

Double Bass – Ian Burt https://www.flickr.com/photos/oddsock/208182066

Guitar – Martin Möller https://en.wikipedia.org/wiki/Guitar#/media/File:GuitareClassique5.png

Harp – Martin Kraft https://commons.wikimedia.org/wiki/File:Harp_Illustration.svg

Ukulele – Arent https://commons.wikimedia.org/wiki/File:Ukulele1.jpg#/media/File:Ukulele1.jpg

Banjo – Dmacks https://en.wikipedia.org/wiki/Banjo#/media/File:BluegrassBanjo.jpg

Flute - ClkerFreeVectorImages https://pixabay.com/en/flute-music-classic-jazz-play-306396/

Oboe - ClkerFreeVectorImages https://pixabay.com/p-34796

Clarinet - ClkerFreeVectorImages https://pixabay.com/p-31372

Bassoon – Celtic_Minstrel https://en.wikipedia.org/wiki/File:BassoonRotated.jpg

French Horn – Fluteflute https://en.wikipedia.org/wiki/French_horn#/media/File:French_horn_front.png

Trumpet – PJ https://commons.wikimedia.org/wiki/File:Trumpet_1.png

Trombone - ClkerFreeVectorImages https://pixabay.com/en/trombone-brass-musician-mouthpiece-25688/

Tuba - Open Clip Art Library https://commons.wikimedia.org/wiki/File:Tuba_01.svg

Xylophone - ClkerFreeVectorImages https://pixabay.com/en/xylophone-sticcado-instrument-music-308025/

Glockenspiel - flamurai https://commons.wikimedia.org/wiki/File:Glockenspiel-malletech.jpg

Tubular Bells – Xylosmygame https://simple.wikipedia.org/wiki/Tubular_bells#/media/File:Deagan_chimes.jpg

Timpani – vxla https://commons.wikimedia.org/wiki/File:Lefima_Timpani.jpg

Bass drum – Open Clip Art Library https://commons.wikimedia.org/wiki/File:Bass_drum.svg

Snare Drum – Vladimir Morozov https://commons.wikimedia.org/wiki/File:Snare_drum_-_Vladimir_Morozov.jpg

Tom toms – ZooFari https://en.wikipedia.org/wiki/Tom-tom_drum#/media/File:TomTom.JPG

Cymbal - Stephan Czuratis https://en.wikipedia.org/wiki/Cymbal#/media/File:2006-07-06_Crash_Zildjian_14.jpg

Piano – Steinway & Sons https://commons.wikimedia.org/wiki/File:Steinway_%26_Sons_concert_grand_piano,_model_D-274,_manufactured_at_Steinway%27s_factory_in_Hamburg,_Germany.png

Harpsichord – FREYmanagement https://en.wikipedia.org/wiki/List_of_period_instruments#/media/File:Harpsichord_VitalJulianFrey.jpg

Organ – Joe Mabel https://commons.wikimedia.org/wiki/File:Wesleyan_University_-_Memorial_Chapel_organ_05.jpg

Celesta – Museumsinsulaner https://commons.wikimedia.org/wiki/File:Celesta_Schiedmayer_MIM_1592.jpg

Electric Guitar – Spike78 https://commons.wikimedia.org/wiki/File:Electric_Guitar_(Superstrat_based_on_ESP_KH_-_vertical)_-_with_hint_lines_and_numbers.png#/media/File:Electric_Guitar_(Superstrat_based_on_ESP_KH_-_vertical).png

Bass Guitar – Itsthatemo https://en.wikipedia.org/wiki/Bass_guitar#/media/File:Stingray_guitar.jpg

Synthesiser – Torley https://commons.wikimedia.org/wiki/File:Roland_V-Synth.png

Saxophone - ↶ https://commons.wikimedia.org/wiki/File:Saxophone_alto2.png

Hands on keyboard – author's photo

Elements of Music

Aim of project
- To become familiar with the seven elements of music (pitch, rhythm, dynamics, tempo, timbre, texture, structure) through performing, composing and listening

Lesson structure
1. Rhythm
2. Pitch
3. Texture
4. Tempo and Dynamics
5. Structure
6. Composing
7. Instruments
8. Conclusion

    Extra Activity: Musical Happy Families

Subject-specific vocabulary
- Rhythm - crotchets, quavers, dotted crotchets and minims
- Pitch – higher, lower, range, step, leap, phrase, melodic shape
- Texture – monophonic, homophonic, polyphonic, heterophonic
- Tempo - Allegro – fast, Allegretto – quite fast, Moderato – medium, Andante – walking pace, Lento – slow, accelerando (accel.) – getting faster, ritardando (rit.) – get slower
- Dynamics - fortissimo (ff) – very loud, forte (f) – loud, mezzo-forte (mf) – medium loud, mezzo piano (mp) – medium soft, Piano (p) – soft, Pianissimo (pp) – very soft, crescendo (cresc.) – getting louder, diminuendo (dim.) – getting softer
- Structure – phrases A, B, C etc.
- Instruments – plucked/bowed strings, woodwind, brass, pitched/unpitched, percussion, others
- Performing, Composing and Listening

Assessments
- Performing – keyboard performance of 'Ode to Joy'
- Composing – keyboard piece using six elements of music
- Listening – Rhythmic and melodic dictation; exercises on texture, structure and instruments

Lesson 1 – Rhythm

Objective
- To differentiate between long and short notes (crotchets, quavers, dotted crotchets and minims)

Resources
- Whiteboard and marker
- Pupils' workbooks and pencils

Procedure

Starter – composing own name rhythms (10 minutes)
- Pupils stand in a circle and march on spot to create steady pulse.
- In turn they say their first name and surname in the space of exactly four beats each. The teacher explains that this is a RHYTHM.
- The pupils clap the rhythm of their names as they say them, then without saying their names.

Main 1 – performing other name rhythms (15 minutes)
- The teacher chooses 5 pupils from the register whose names all have different four-beat rhythms. The pupils stand in a line at the front of the class facing the rest of the pupils. The teacher writes the pupils' first names and surnames on the whiteboard, separating the syllables with dashes. The rest of the class chant the names in order, trying to make the names as rhythmic as possible.
- The teacher writes the four-beat rhythm for each name above the name using a combination of crotchets, quavers, dotted crotchets and minims, explaining what a rhythm is and how long each note is. The rest of the class claps and chants the names simultaneously.
- The teacher rubs out the names, but leaves the rhythms on the whiteboard. The five chosen pupils sit down with the rest of the class. The whole class claps the rhythms in order.
- The teacher numbers the rhythms 1-5. The teacher holds up 1-5 fingers and counts the class in '1-2-3-4'. The class should then clap the correct rhythm.
- The teacher repeats the previous step with individual pupils.

Main 2 – listening to other name rhythms (20 minutes)
- The teacher explains that the pupils are going to play a game where they identify the correct rhythm 10 times. First, there is a practice. The teacher claps twice one of the 5 rhythms on the board. The pupils hold up, in front of their chests, the correct number of fingers (1-5) for the clapped rhythm.
- Repeat the previous step 5 times, this time with the pupils scoring 1 for the correct rhythm (first time) and 0 for the incorrect rhythm. They keep their score in their head.
- The teacher announces that rhythms 6-10 will be based on *two* rhythms (which could be the same). The teacher claps the two rhythms without a gap between them. This time, the pupils have to hold up *two* hands to show the correct rhythm. They score 2 if both hands are correct, 1 if one hand is correct, or 0 if neither are correct.
- At the end of the game, the teacher asks pupils' scores out of 15.

Plenary – rhythmic dictation (15 minutes)
- The teacher distributes workbooks – pupils name their books on page 1 then turn to listening exercise on page 2. Teacher claps each rhythm (including the example) twice – see rhythms on next page. The pupils write down the rhythm and hand them in for marking at the end of the lesson.

Elements of Music – Teacher's Guide page 4

Rhythmic dictation
Teacher's copy for clapping and marking

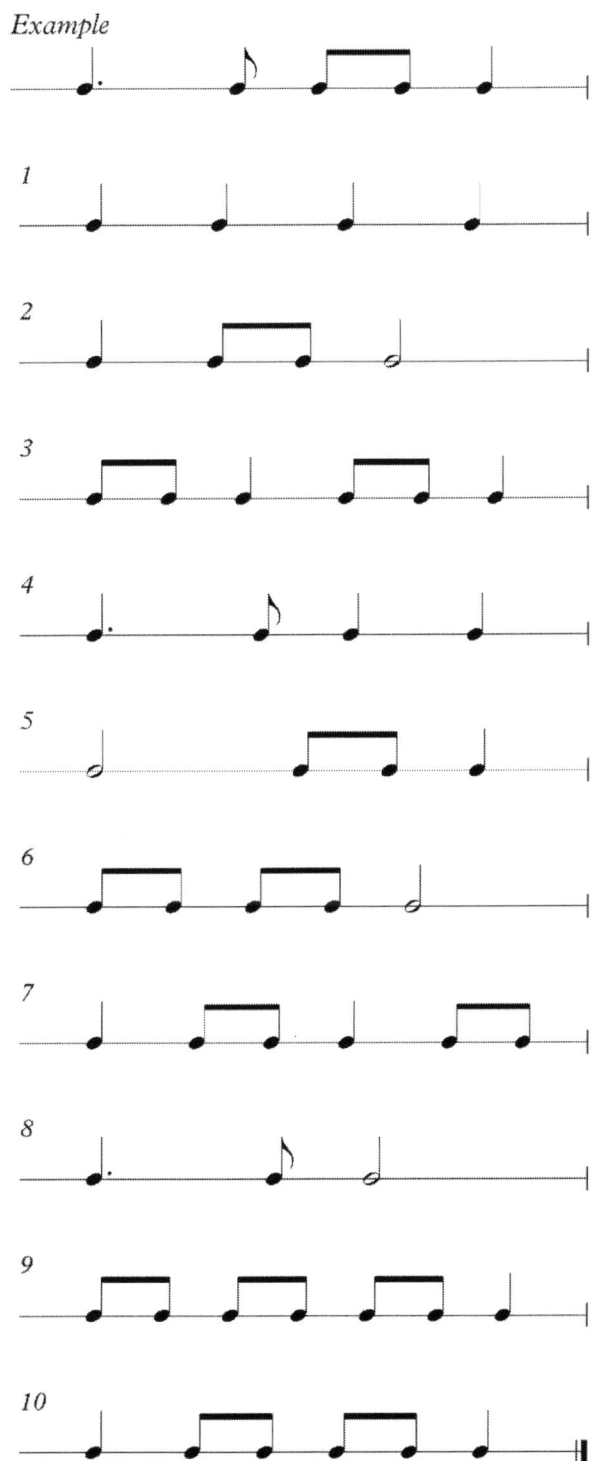

Elements of Music – Teacher's Guide page 5

Lesson 2 – Pitch

Objective
- All pupils differentiate between high and low notes
- Many pupils identify whether one note is higher, lower or the same as another
- Some pupils identify the melodic shape of a short conjunct phrase

Resources
- Pupils' workbooks
- Keyboards and headphones

Procedure

Starter – Chanting and singing 'Ode to Joy' (10 minutes)
- Pupils copy the teacher chant the English words for 'Ode to Joy', noting the rhythms
- Pupils learn to sing the melody of 'Ode to Joy'

Main 1 – Pitch dictation – listening (20 minutes)
- On page 3 of workbooks, pupils write out the melody played or sung by the teacher one bar at a time, by working out whether each note is higher than, lower than or the same as the previous one. The melody should stay within the range of the five notes CDEFG given at the top of the sheet
- Pupils should note that the melody is mostly made up of steps (the few leaps are already given on the sheet). The melody also has a recognisable shape if the 'dots' were to be joined: for example, the 1st, 2nd and 4th phrases all go smoothly up, down, up and down
- Pupils should copy the rhythms, using crotchets, dotted crotchets, quavers and minims
- When finished, pupils check their work with the printed melody on page 4 of workbook

Main 2 – Performing on the keyboard (20 minutes)
- In pairs, pupils learn to play the melody (right hand only) of 'Ode to Joy' with their right hand from page 4 of workbook
- More advanced pupils can start to learn the left hand as well

Plenary – Performing on the keyboard (10 minutes)
- Some pupils perform their work-in-progress to the rest of the class

Elements of Music – Teacher's Guide page 6

Lesson 3 – Texture

Objectives
- All pupils differentiate between a single melodic line and more than one line
- Some pupils identify whether the texture is single melody, melody and accompaniment or several melodies
- A few pupils use subject-specific words to describe texture: monophonic, homophonic, polyphonic or heterophonic

Resources
- Pupils' workbooks
- 6-minute video about Musical Texture: https://www.youtube.com/watch?v=_J2R20X16Jc
- Musical Texture quiz playlist: https://www.youtube.com/playlist?list=PLnvmFAu748V58ihHKDwFkG6kyXwxNvtQ4

Procedure

Starter – listening to texture in 'Ode to Joy' (10 minutes)
- Teacher plays through 'Ode to Joy' with both hands. Pupils answer the question: 'What has been added to the melody since last lesson?' (Notes in the left hand.) The teacher explains that this is a change in TEXTURE.
- Teacher plays 'Ode to Joy' with both hands again. This time, pupils are encouraged by the teacher describe the TEXTURE of each 4-bar phrase along these lines:
    1. single melodic line   2. another version of the melody played at the same time
    3. two tunes together   4. melody and accompaniment

Main 1 – listening to different textures (20 minutes)
- Pupils watch and listen to 6-minute video about Musical Texture, learning about different kinds of texture: monophonic, homophonic, polyphonic and heterophonic ('biphonic' is also covered, but this can be ignored for the purposes of this lesson)
- Pupils complete Musical Texture quiz on page 6 of workbooks. Answers as follows:
    1. Gregorian chant - monophonic
    2. Lonesome valley - heterophonic
    3. Carmen overture - homophonic
    4. Bach cello suite – monophonic
    5. Shostakovich fugue - polyphonic
    6. Indian classical music - heterophonic
    7. Unomathemba - homophonic
    8. Don't Be So Hard on Yourself - homophonic

Main 2 – performing 'Ode to Joy' with different textures (20 minutes)
- Pupils practise as much of 'Ode to Joy' from page 4 of workbooks as they can with the (increasingly challenging) variety of textures provided by the left hand. If they are not able to play hands together at all, they should continue to practise the right hand melody by itself.

Plenary - performing 'Ode to Joy' with different textures (10 minutes)
- One or two pupils play each of the four phrases of 'Ode to Joy', thus demonstrating the different textures (monophonic, heterophonic, polyphonic and homophonic)

Elements of Music – Teacher's Guide page 7

Lesson 4 – Tempo and Dynamics

Objectives
- All pupils differentiate between fast/slow and loud/soft
- Most pupils identify gradual changes in tempo and dynamics: getting faster/slower, louder/softer
- Some pupils use Italian words to describe tempo and dynamics

Resources
- 'In the Hall of the Mountain King' https://www.youtube.com/watch?v=xrIYT-MrVaI
- Keyboards (one between two)
- Sheet music for 'Ode to Joy'

Procedure

Starter – Listening to tempo and dynamics (5 minutes)
- Teacher plays 'In the Hall of the Mountain King'. What changes occur during the piece? (It gradually becomes faster and louder.)

Main 1 – Understanding tempo and dynamics (10 minutes)
- On page 7 of workbooks, pupils write five Italian words for tempo in order from slow to fast
- Pupils discuss and write down the meaning of 'accelerando' and 'ritardando'
- Pupils work out what the dynamic markings (pp-ff) signify
- Pupils discuss and write down the meaning of 'crescendo' and 'diminuendo'
- The following musical terms are used on page 7 of the workbook:
    - TEMPO Allegro – fast, Allegretto – quite fast, Moderato – medium, Andante – walking pace, Lento – slow, accelerando (accel.) – getting faster, ritardando (rit.) – get slower
    - DYNAMICS fortissimo (ff) – very loud, forte (f) – loud, mezzo-forte (mf) – medium loud, mezzo piano (mp) – medium soft, Piano (p) – soft, Pianissimo (pp) – very soft, crescendo (cresc.) – getting louder, diminuendo (dim.) – getting softer

Main 2 – Performing on the keyboard with tempo and dynamics (25 minutes)
- Pupils practise as much of 'Ode to Joy' as they can with the (increasingly challenging) variety of textures provided by the left hand. If they are not able to play hands together at all, they should continue to practise the right hand melody by itself.

Plenary - performing 'Ode to Joy' with tempo and dynamics (20 minutes)
- All pupils play as much of 'Ode to Joy' as they are able, incorporating the differences in pitch, rhythm, texture, tempo and dynamics
- Teacher assesses the keyboard performance

Assessments for interim grades
1. Rhythm dictation (lesson 1)
2. Melodic dictation (lesson 2)
3. Listening exercise on Texture (lesson 3)
4. Keyboard performance (lesson 4)

Lesson 5 – Structure

Objectives
- All pupils recognise repetition and contrast in a piece of music
- Most pupils identify the phrase structure of a section of music (e.g. AABA)
- Some pupils identify slight variations in repeated phrases (e.g. AA_1BA_1)

Resources
- Pupils' workbooks
- Piano
- Coldplay – 'Clocks' https://www.youtube.com/watch?v=d020hcWA_Wg
- 'Down by the Salley Gardens' (Irish folk song) https://www.youtube.com/watch?v=027ZJX5XVjs
- 'The Elephant' from *The Carnival of the Animals* by Saint-Saëns
  https://www.youtube.com/watch?v=VZAGLJtj5RU

Procedure

Starter: Listening to the phrase structure in 'Ode to Joy' (10 minutes)
- Teacher (or confident pupil) plays the right-hand melody of 'Ode to Joy' on the piano while the pupils follow the score. Which phrases are more or less the same? (The 1st, 2nd and 4th.) Which one is different? (The 3rd.) Are there any slight differences in the similar phrases? (Yes – the last bar of the 1st phrase is different from the last bar of the 2nd and 4th phrase. The 1st phrase feels 'unfinished' but the 2nd and 4th phrases feel 'finished'.)
- Teacher explains that the STRUCTURE of a piece can be described by giving each phrase a letter of the alphabet starting with A, using the same letter for similar phrases and the next letter in the alphabet for different phrases. 'Ode to Joy' can be described as having the structure AABA. (An even more detailed description is AA_1BA_1, because of the slight variations between the A sections.)

Main 1: Listening to the phrase structure in other pieces (10 minutes)
- On page 8 of workbooks, pupils identify the phrase structure in the first section of the following pieces (disregarding the introductions):
  - Coldplay – 'Clocks' (AAAA)
  - 'Down by the Salley Gardens' (Irish folk song) (AABA)
  - 'The Elephant' from *The Carnival of the Animals* by Saint-Saëns (ABA_1C)

Main 2: Composing a melody using a chosen structure (30 minutes)
- Pupils now begin composing their keyboard piece for their music exam on page 10 of their workbooks. Using 'Ode to Joy' as a model, the piece should have the following:
  - RHYTHM: melody uses crotchets, dotted crotchets, quavers and minims
  - PITCH: melody uses the notes CDEFG; mainly stepwise; recognisable shape
  - STRUCTURE: Four four-bar phrases in 4/4 time; A clear phrase structure that has both repetition and contrast

Plenary – Performing composition on the keyboard (10 minutes)
- Some pupils play their work-in-progress to the rest of the class (if they prefer, the teacher can play it). Does their piece have all the features listed above?

Elements of Music – Teacher's Guide page 9

Lesson 6 – Composing

Objectives
- All pupils compose a piece of music showing some variety in the elements of music
- Most pupils compose a piece showing a variety of rhythm, pitch, texture, tempo, dynamics and structure
- Some pupils exploit the elements of music in a subtle and expressive way, for example with a slight variation in melody or a well-placed crescendo

Resources
- 'Ode to Joy' sheet music (one per pupil)
- Composition worksheet (one per pupil)
- Keyboards and headphones

Procedure

Starter – Listening to six elements of music in 'Ode to Joy' (5 minutes)
- Teacher (or confident pupil) plays 'Ode to Joy' with both hands on the piano while the pupils follow the score. What are the six elements of music contained in this piece? (Rhythm, pitch, texture, tempo, dynamics and structure.)

Main – Composing using six elements of music (45 minutes)
- Pupils continue the composing project on page 10 of their workbooks. Using 'Ode to Joy' as a model, the piece should have the following (the first three were already discussed last lesson):
  - RHYTHM: melody uses crotchets, dotted crotchets, quavers and minims
  - PITCH: melody uses the notes CDEFG; mainly stepwise; recognisable shape
  - STRUCTURE: four four-bar phrases in 4/4 time; A clear phrase structure that has both repetition and contrast
  - TEXTURE: notes in the left hand using the notes CDEFG and crotchets, dotted crotchets, quavers and minims providing a variety of texture (monophonic, heterophonic, polyphonic, homophonic)
  - DYNAMICS: markings such as p, f and cresc.
  - TEMPO: markings such as Allegro and rit.

Plenary – Performing composition on the keyboard (10 minutes)
- Some pupils play their work-in-progress to the rest of the class (if they prefer, the teacher can play it). Does their piece have all the features listed above?

Elements of Music – Teacher's Guide page 10

Lesson 7 – Instruments

Objectives
- All pupils differentiate between broad types of instrument (wind, strings, percussion, other)
- Many pupils identify more specific families: bowed/plucked strings, woodwind/brass, pitched/unpitched percussion, keyboard/pop & jazz
- Some pupils identify specific instruments and voice types: violin, electric guitar, flute, trumpet, xylophone, etc.

Resources
- Pupils' workbooks
- 5 packs of instrument cards – each pack has 32 cards with the name and picture of an instrument
- Musical Instrument audio examples:
  http://www.musictechteacher.com/music_learning_theory/music_instruments.htm

Procedure

Starter: instruments - appraising (10 minutes)
- The teacher divides the whiteboard into 8 equal sections, labelled as follows:

STRINGS	WIND	PERCUSSION	OTHER
Plucked	Woodwind	Pitched	Keyboard
Bowed	Brass	Unpitched	Pop & Jazz

- Pupils suggest instruments which the teacher writes into the relevant box.
- Pupils complete the table on page 9 of their workbooks.

Main: instruments – appraising/listening (20 minutes)
- The teacher rubs out the instruments (but not the section headings) and divides the pupils into groups of 3-4 – they sit on the carpet. The teacher gives a pack of instrument cards to each group.
- The groups must work together to divide the instrument cards equally amongst the 8 'families' of instruments, in the same layout as on the whiteboard. Which group can divide them up first?
- Led by the teacher, the class discusses the differences between the instruments within each family, particularly in relation to PITCH (e.g. the violin is the highest and the double bass is the lowest bowed string instrument).
- The teacher plays Musical Instrument audio examples from the weblink.

Plenary – Composing using all seven elements of music (30 minutes)
- Pupils continue the composing project on page 10 of their workbooks. In addition to the six elements of music listed in the last lesson, the pupils should now choose an instrument for the beginning of the piece and another instrument from a different family later in the piece.

Elements of Music – Teacher's Guide page 11

Lesson 8 - Conclusion

Objectives
- To demonstrate knowledge of families and instruments
- To finish composing a piece which demonstrates all seven elements of music

Resources
- Pupils' workbooks
- 5 packs of instrument cards – each pack has 32 cards with the name and picture of an instrument
- Musical Instrument Quiz: https://www.youtube.com/watch?v=d4S3yXtAC9Y

Procedure

Starter: Musical Instrument Quiz - listening (10 minutes)
- Pupils turn to page 12 of their workbooks
- The teacher plays the Musical Instrument Quiz (also showing the video, so that the numbers of the questions are clear)
- In the table on page 12 of their workbooks., the pupils write their 20 answers to the Music Instrument Quiz
- The exercise is marked out of 40 - half a mark if Family is not specific (i.e. strings/wind/percussion/other); half a mark if instrument itself is not spelled correctly

Number	Family	Instrument
1	Other (½) / Pop & Jazz (1)	Saxophone
2	Other (½) / Keyboard (1)	Piano
3	Wind (½) / Woodwind (1)	Flute
4	Other (½) / Keyboard (1)	Harpsichord
5	Strings (½) / Bowed Strings (1)	Cello
6	Wind (½) / Brass (1)	Tuba
7	Strings (½) / Bowed Strings (1)	Viola
8	Percussion (½) / Unpitched percussion (1)	Cymbal
9	Percussion (½) / Unpitched percussion (1)	Triangle
10	Wind (½) / Brass (1)	French Horn
11	Other (½) / Keyboard (1)	Organ
12	Strings (½) / Plucked Strings (1)	Guitar
13	Wind (½) / Brass (1)	Trumpet
14	Strings (½) / Bowed Strings (1)	Violin
15	Wind (½) / Brass (1)	Trombone
16	Wind (½) / Woodwind (1)	Oboe
17	Strings (½) / Plucked Strings (1)	Harp
18	Wind (½) / Woodwind (1)	Bassoon
19	Strings (½) / Bowed Strings (1)	Double Bass
20	Wind (½) / Woodwind (1)	Flute

Main: Composing (40 minutes)
- Pupils complete their keyboard compositions demonstrating all seven elements of music.

Plenary: Performing compositions (10 minutes)
- Some pupils perform their composition to the rest of the class; other compositions are played by the teacher

Elements of Music – Teacher's Guide page 12

Extra Activity: Musical Happy Families

An optional extra activity using the instrument cards

- The teacher divides the pupils into groups of 3-4 – they sit on the carpet. The teacher gives a pack of instrument cards to each group.
- The teacher explains the rules of the Musical Happy Families card game:
    - One pupil in each group is chosen to be the dealer. The dealer shuffles and deals the cards.
    - The pupils pick up their cards but MUST NOT show the other pupils.
    - The dealer is the first pupil to ask ONE other pupil in the group, do you have the [instrument] from the [family], e.g. 'Do you have the harp from the plucked string family?'
    - If the other pupil DOES have the card, they hand it to the first pupil, who then has another turn.
    - If the other pupil DOES NOT have the card, it is their turn.
    - When a pupil has a whole family of four cards, they place the four cards face-up in front of them.
    - The person with the most families when all the cards are used up OR when the teacher stops the game is the winner within that group.

Families of instruments

as categorised in the card game

A. Bowed strings
1. Violin
2. Viola
3. Cello
4. Double Bass

B. Plucked strings
1. Acoustic Guitar
2. Harp
3. Ukulele
4. Banjo

C. Woodwind
1. Flute
2. Oboe
3. Clarinet
4. Bassoon

D. Brass
1. French Horn
2. Trumpet
3. Trombone
4. Tuba

E. Pitched percussion
1. Xylophone
2. Glockenspiel
3. Tubular Bells
4. Timpani

F. Unpitched percussion
1. Bass drum
2. Snare Drum
3. Tom toms
4. Cymbal

G. Keyboards
1. Piano
2. Harpsichord
3. Organ
4. Celesta

H. Pop & Jazz
1. Electric Guitar
2. Bass Guitar
3. Synthesiser
4. Saxophone

Notes

Elements of Music

Pupil's Workbook

Name.. Class........

Rhythm *a pattern of long and short notes*

♩ is called a **crotchet** and lasts for 1 beat

♪ is called a ……………………………… and lasts for ………. beats

♩. is called a ……………………………… and lasts for ………. beats

♪ is called a ……………………………… and lasts for ………. a beat

Listening quiz
Write down the rhythms you hear clapped.

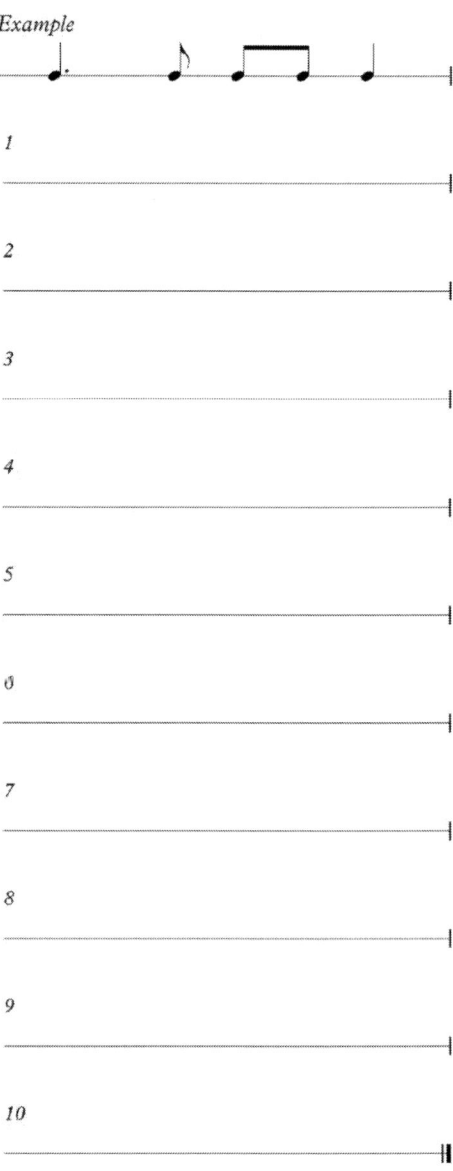

Pupil's Workbook page 2

Pitch *high and low notes*

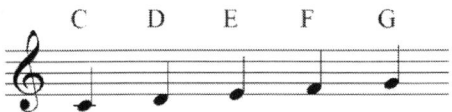

Range how many notes in a melody (tune) from the lowest to the highest note. Most of 'Ode to Joy' uses a range of five notes (apart from the low G at the end of the third line):

Step when two notes in a melody are next to one another on the keyboard. Most of 'Ode to Joy' is made up of steps.

Leap when two notes in a melody are wider apart than a step. Two leaps are already notated on the third line below.

Phrase a section of melody that can be sung in one breath. 'Ode to Joy' is made up of four phrases, each one four bars long.

Melodic shape the shape made by the melody if you were to join the 'dots'. For example, the first phrase below goes smoothly up, down, up and down.

Learn to sing 'Ode to Joy, then write out the melody one bar at a time, by working out whether each note is higher than, lower than or the same as the previous one.

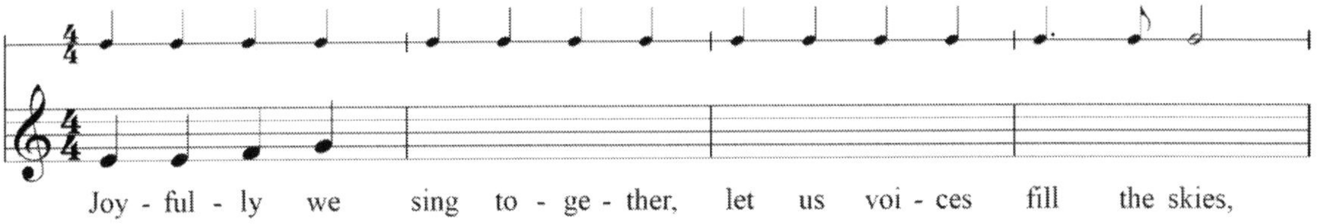

Joy - ful - ly we sing to - ge - ther, let us voi - ces fill the skies,

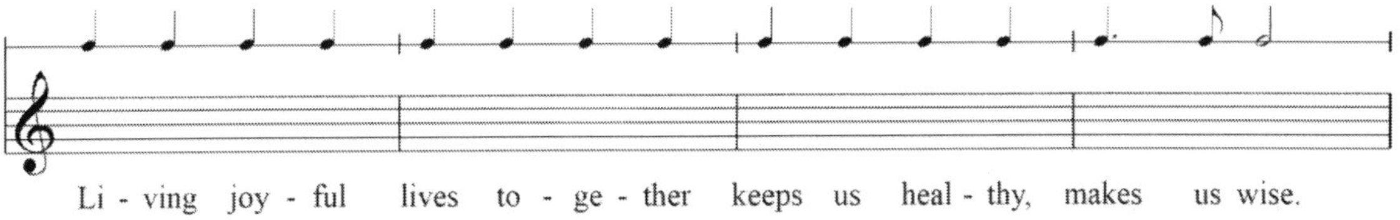

Li - ving joy - ful lives to - ge - ther keeps us heal - thy, makes us wise.

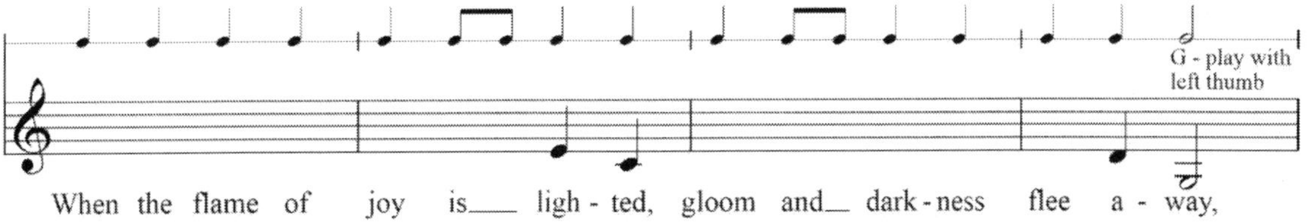

When the flame of joy is___ ligh - ted, gloom and___ dark - ness flee a - way,

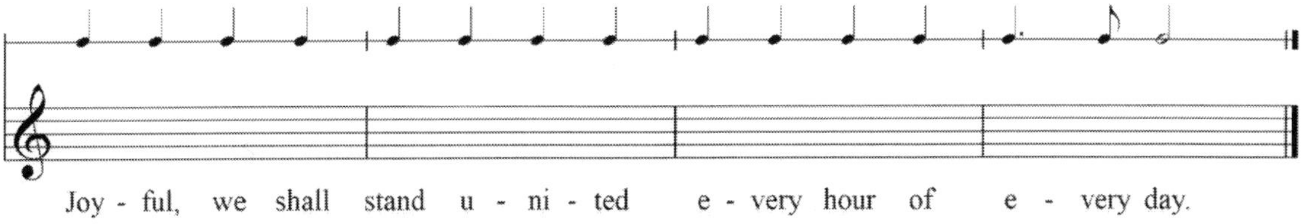

G - play with left thumb

Joy - ful, we shall stand u - ni - ted e - very hour of e - very day.

Pupil's Workbook page 3

Performing project

Ode to Joy

Moderato

f Joy-ful-ly we sing to-ge-ther, let us voi-ces fill the skies,

Li-ving joy-ful lives to-ge-ther keeps us heal-thy, makes us wise.

p When the flame of joy is ligh-ted, gloom and dark-ness flee a-way,

rit.

ff Joy-ful, we shall stand u-ni-ted e-very hour of e-very day.

Pupil's Workbook page 4

Performing project – assessment

Use this checklist to help you practise. The assessment will be completed by the teacher.

Element	Question	Tick
Rhythm	Are the crotchets played correctly?	
	Are the dotted crotchets played correctly?	
	Are the quavers played correctly?	
	Are the minims played correctly?	
	Is a steady sense of beat kept throughout the piece?	
Pitch	Are all the different fingers of the right hand used to play the notes CDEFG?	
	Are most of the steps played correctly?	
	Are most of the leaps played correctly?	
	Are the melodic shapes broadly correct?	
Texture	Is the heterophonic texture in line 2 played correctly?	
	Is the polyphonic texture in line 3 played correctly?	
	Is the homophonic texture in line 4 played correctly?	
Dynamics	Is the 'forte' dynamic marking in line 1 observed?	
	Is the crescendo in line 2 observed?	
	Is the 'piano' dynamic marking in line 3 observed?	
	Is the 'fortissimo' dynamic marking in line 4 observed?	
	Is there at least on Is the 'forte' dynamic marking in line 1 observed?	
Tempo	Is the piece played at a 'moderato' tempo?	
	Is the tempo maintained throughout the piece?	
	Is the 'rit.' observed towards the end?	

TOTAL out of 20

Texture *how the voices and/or instruments fit together*

Monophonic - unaccompanied melody (could be performed by more than one person)
Homophonic - melody and chords
Polyphonic - several tunes at once
Heterophonic - variations of same tune played at the same time

Listening quiz
Listen to ten extracts of music and write down which of the four words above best describes the texture.

Number	Title	Texture
1	Gregorian chant	
2	Lonesome valley	
3	Carmen overture	
4	Bach cello suite	
5	Shostakovitch fugue	
6	Indian classical music	
7	Unomathemba	
8	Don't Be So Hard on Yourself	

Tempo *how fast or slow the music is*

Here are five Italian words describing tempo:

Allegretto	Andante	Allegro	Lento	Moderato
quite fast	*walking pace*	*Fast*	*slow*	*Medium pace*

Now write them in order, from the slowest to the fastest:

Slowest >>> Fastest

Can you work out the meaning of these two Italian words describing tempo?

Accelerando (accel.) ……………………………………………………………

Ritardando (rit.)……………………………………………………………..

Dynamics *how loud or soft the music is*

We use the first letter of each these Italian words to describe dynamics.

    forte – loud

    piano – soft

    mezzo – medium

When the letter is doubled, it means 'very' loud or soft.

Write the ENGLISH description of each dynamic marking below.

pp	*p*	*mp*	*mf*	*f*	F*f*

Can you work out the meaning of these two Italian words describing dynamics?

crescendo (cresc.) ……………………………………………………………

diminuendo (dim.) ……………………………………………………………

Structure *the order of the sections in a piece of music*

You can use capital letters A, B, C and so on to describe the sections in a piece. 'Ode to Joy' can be described as having the structure AABA. You can also use small numbers to show a similar section that has been changed slightly, for example A_1, which means a slightly different version of A.

Listening quiz

Listen to the first section of each of the following pieces, ignoring any introductions.

Write down using letters (and possibly numbers) the structure of the phrases in each piece.

The first one is done for you.

Number	Title	Structure
1	Ode to Joy	A A_1 B A_1
2	Clocks	
3	Down by the Salley Gardens	
4	The Elephant	

Instruments

Write the instruments below in the correct box in the grid, from highest to lowest pitched.

STRINGS	WIND	PERCUSSION	OTHER
Plucked	**Woodwind**	**Pitched**	**Keyboard**
Bowed	**Brass**	**Unpitched**	**Pop & Jazz**

Harp	Bassoon	Piano	Tom toms
Tuba	Saxophone	Trombone	Cello
Viola	Bass drum	Cymbal	Electric Guitar
Snare Drum	Acoustic Guitar	Trumpet	Xylophone
Glockenspiel	Harpsichord	Ukulele	Clarinet
Synthesiser	Double Bass	Oboe	Celesta
French Horn	Organ	Tubular Bells	Bass Guitar
Flute	Timpani	Banjo	Violin

Composing project

Using 'Ode to Joy' as a model, compose a piece for the keyboard that shows a contrast in all seven elements of music. For more details, see the assessment criteria opposite.

Pupil's Workbook page 10

Composing project: assessment

Use this checklist to help you compose. The assessment will be completed by the teacher.

Element	Question	Tick
Rhythm	Does the melody use a variety of note-lengths?	
	Are most rhythms correctly notated?	
	Do most of the bars add up to four beats?	
	Is there a longer note at the end of each line (phrase)?	
Pitch	Does the melody use all the notes CDEFG?	
	Are most pitches correctly notated?	
	Is the melody mainly made up of steps?	
	Does the melody have a recognisable shape within each phrase?	
Structure	Does the piece divide into four phrases, one on each line?	
	Is at least one phrase similar to a previous one?	
	Is at least one phrase different from a previous one?	
Texture	Does the piece begin with a recognisable texture?	
	Is there a contrast of texture within the piece?	
Dynamics	Is there a dynamic marking at the beginning such as f or p?	
	Is there at least one other dynamic marking in the piece?	
	Is a crescendo and/or diminuendo marking used?	
Tempo	Is there a tempo marking at the beginning?	
	Is there at least one other tempo marking in the piece?	
Instrument	Is there an instrument specified at the beginning?	
	Is an instrument from a different family specified later in the piece?	

TOTAL out of 20

Pupil's Workbook page 11

Musical Instrument Quiz

Listen to twenty instruments (1-20) and write their family and name below.

Number	Family	Instrument
1		
2		
3		
4		
5		
6		
7		
8		
9		
10		
11		
12		
13		
14		
15		
16		
17		
18		
19		
20		

TOTAL out of 40

Printed in Great Britain
by Amazon.co.uk, Ltd.,
Marston Gate.